BOOK OF TRUTHS

BRANDON "AMAYZN" NELSON

PenFire Publishing
Kansas City, MO
penfirepublishing.com

Copyright © 2022 by Brandon "Amayzn" Nelson

All rights reserved. No part of this book may be reproduced, scanned, or distributed in any printed or electronic form, including information storage and retrieval systems, without permission. Please do not participate in or encourage piracy of copyrighted materials in violation of the author's rights.

Please purchase only authorized editions.

First Edition: April 2022

ISBN: 978-1-952838-10-1

This book is a work of fiction. Names, characters, places, dates, and incidents

are products of the author's imagination or are used fictitiously, satirically, or as parody. Any resemblance to actual persons, living or dead, business establishments, events, or locales is entirely coincidental.

10 9 8 7 7 5 4 3 3 1

Design, Layout, Edits: Sheri Hall & Brooke Hawkins

DEDICATION

Without my grandmother,
The things most important to me
I would not have.

My taste for life,
Appreciation of family,
Understanding of love,
This thing called poetry,
And a relationship with Christ.

Ethyl Jean Nelson,
In your memory,
This is for you.

SPECIAL THANKS

To my mom, DeNeese Nelson, for always being my toughest critic and my biggest supporter both in the brightest and darkest times.

To my mentors, Bonafyde G and The Recipe, who taught me how to find my voice.

To God who loves me, keeps me, and allows me to STILL find the words to write.

To the countless family and friends that push me to be as best I can be and beyond.

And last but not least, to Sheri Hall and Poetry for Personal Power, thank you for helping me become not just a better writer, but a much better person. Thank you for helping me achieve something I never dreamt I would. I encourage anyone to look them up and discover the beauty of both poetry and mental health.

I love you and thank you.

TABLE OF CONTENTS

Dedication 5
Special Thanks 6
The Truth About ~~Love~~ 9
    How I Got This Scar 11
    Confidential 14
    4 Letters 16
The Truth About Manhood 19
    Childish Things 21
    Men Don't Cry 24
    Bigger Than Standards 26
    Bear My Cross 27
The Truth About My Words 29
    I Can't 31
    Then What 33
    November 18th 36
Bio 39

THE TRUTH ABOUT ~~LOVE~~

"Love's gonna get you killed.
But prides gonna be the death of you and you and me and you…"

Bēkon from Kendrick Lamar's "PRIDE."

HOW I GOT THIS SCAR

> Now that she's moved on,
> I finally listened to her song.

I wish
I could put my heart
In water and let it re-rock
That place you used to belong.
Maybe I lack the body armor
Supplement to heal brokenness.

I wish
I could revisit the well
And not find it dry.
I wish to revisit a place
That was Heaven
In pink and white.

I wish
I could finish
The bottles you bought me
But all I taste is bittersweet.
The memories never wash away,
Though I wish they did.

I wish
Your smile didn't hurt so much.
I wish my skin could
deprogram from your touch
So I could move on
The way you did,

> *With a text.*

Of all the characters
You used in that message,
None of them were
The one I fell in love with.
The one you were when
You were with me.

I wish
She missed me.
Us.
I wish
Pride wasn't such a demon.
It's more courageous to speak.

                        Do not misunderstand these thoughts.
                            This is not me begging you back.

I wish
You could have
Counted the number of tears
I shed those months.
I did,
There were 841 to be exact.

But number 842 was special.
I wrote a request with it.
My wish came true.
I wished to be okay.
It didn't happen exactly that day
But when it came ...

I wish
You could've been there
To see me come out of that kind of low
That even my pen doesn't fully know.
While I may rue the day you left,
I still wish.

I wish
You could've seen how
The sun shined
When I lifted my head.
How bright and warm
Its hug felt.

I remember
How sweet the water was.
How good it was
To sing a wind whistle
Harmoniously, without practice,

On key, on beat.

I remember
Speaking proverbs and psalms
That could soften
Or harden a soul.
I looked,
Wishing I'd see you.

See me,
Not dead,
Not broken,
Still healing.
Not the man you left,
But stronger.

                                        I'd tell you thank you
                              For the lesson I had forgotten.

I just wish you didn't have to break my heart
To remind me I still have one.

CONFIDENTIAL

What's understood doesn't have to be explained.

Can you keep a secret?

I love being in the
Same room with you.
Everybody tryna get close
To figure out your mood.
That smile when you say
"No"
Belongs to me.
You are the motivation
To my song.
We sway to our own melody

No one will ever make my name
Sound sexy as you.
You sit in my chest like a chain
You've got my back all the same.
We know this ain't love.
But it's us,
        And I like it that way.
Same as 1 o'clock
In the morning dates.
        It's gangsta.

You're the pistol I hold close,
        Shotgun in my Impala.
I'll ride for you into the sunset
And you ain't even gave me no ass
        Yet
I know what your heartbeat feels like.
In your eyes,
        My wrongs are right.
We ain't gotta explain shit to nobody.
This is better.

No snaps
No reacts
No questions
Bout him

        In your pics
Or that girl
        In my face
It ain't that,
Won't ever be that.
Only bliss when we kiss.

It turns me on
        How much you
        Love your job.
Keeps me cool
        When I wanna
        Walk out on mine.
You're peaceful as
        Light ice in lemonade.
Dolce and Gabbana Light Blue
        Smells almost as good as you.

I had a million questions
        I wanted to ask
But then I saw you in my t shirt
        And forgot all them shits.
I could watch you
        Scroll and troll
Laughing at the comments.
Only time we mention thirst
Is debating which one is best:
        Crush or Vess?

I only get mad
When I want more of your time
As it escapes with your vapor trail.
I just need you close.
The thought makes me bite
My bottom lip.
I take your hand
Bring you back,
        Remind.
I only tell you to my heart.

...Can you keep a secret?

4 LETTERS

evelyn champagne king
sang once
that kisses don't lie

i'm learning
i need to be kissed
more than i need
drinking water
cold   robust   bold
i don't want pecks
that play like
        instant messages
i want ours to tell a story
of how our mouths
        make love
sensual   sweet   nasty
        passionate
we so lost
we forget our way home
so we start anew right here
this our covenant
i can't get enough of it
i want to touch you in ways
that another language
cannot translate
hands move from hair
to nape   to face
gently dig fingers into thighs
feeling your hands scratch
your name into my back
gives me a high
that i'm unsure how
to come down from
your touch warm as the sun
have i told you
        i want a kiss
that makes me feel
        hungered for
'til my goosebumps and

taste buds find equal
wavelength
and my whole-body screams
what my soul can't
i need that
so don't tease me with
        bad dreams
i want the nightmare
        hiding in you
make me your victim
i your conqueror
tasked to quell a fire
        that burns loud
experiencing your tongue
        as paintbrush
creating art across my
        beard and lips
sucking it to dip in ink
create more masterpieces
i feign for that
        need it
    back to back
i won't get tired of
standing on the edge of lust
before plunging
        into orgasms
we've never experienced
before
until
      we
            clicked
and this is still the best
feeling
all before we take off our
clothes
then die
a wonderful death
are you ready
        don't make me wait

THE TRUTH ABOUT MANHOOD

I feel like letting free
Yet I rebel against my own energy
And choose to be salty without the sea

These cheeks
Will not be the altar
Of wet prayers today

Sheri Purpose Hall "Restraint"

CHILDISH THINGS

One of my biggest flaws
is I take things too literally.
Like when the Good Book said
"But when I became a man,
I put away childish things"
And the day I decided that
I was tired of always feeling
               left behind.
I packed my up Power Rangers,
put these silent partners in a
cardboard box in the corner of
my old room.
I was hoping to ascend to the
heavens of manhood.
Nowhere did it ever say I
needed to put away toys.
And the first thing I did
               was descend.
And the first thing I learned
about being a man
              was poise.
    -Displace tears
    -Face fears
Which is easy when you ain't
scared of shit.
Next was get grip.
        Found my niche.
Pull the baddest with the fattest.
Gritting was my business
And business was good,
              'til it wasn't.
Lost a lot of sleep in the process.
Money is the root of all evil:
jealousy is one of its trees.
Envy, a fruit nobody should eat.
I've destroyed mics and
               broke hearts.
A two timer
         now two times father.
The irony of trying to be a
better man to my daughters

than I ever was to their
mothers.
And for all this confidence I
own, I have also developed
                      insecurities.
Excelling increased doubts and
made me afraid to fail.
Now the number of times I've
called Gods name is equivalent
to the number I've made
          women say mine.
I'm on my 7th or 8th second
chance; It comes with the
territory of calling myself a man.
But no matter how zipped I am
into this code,
there's a place in 64128 that
          I still call home.
I go there from time to time.
Even when they change the
color of the house,
there's always this little boy
waiting and watching in the
window.
Wanting to see if I'll be brave
enough to knock at the door,
forever vigilant.
He reminds me of myself.
          His smile infectious.
This one time I watched him.
In his front yard clutching
broken branches governing his
territory, chest high. '90s pop
          culture personified.
He kicks and swings into non-
existence conditioning to
combat demons he has
          not yet seen.
He is more ears than muscle but
his heart is astounding, living
the good life even as
          sirens surround him.
I want to tell him so badly
          little boy

remain a toys r us kind of kid.
Waterfalls are not
          worth chasing.
You'll learn about rivers and the
lakes so cherish the
      brush and the creek.
Your only job right now is to be
        Tommy.
Even if you ain't aware that you
in the middle of a
      power struggle.
Even if your teammates change.
This life stresses so much about
wrong and right,
      black and white.
      a lot of red between.
Truth be told the best to
      remain green.
So future king
      don't lose your square.
Keep your joy.
      Appreciate your love.
Never bow.
God if I only knew then
      what I know now.
And so I do what most black
men don't do anymore.
        I reach out.
Hug him.
      Close the gap.
But like communication these
days,
      we are hit and miss.
We can feel but cant see,
      hidden in mist.
We are transparent as the truth.
I hope I never see him lose
      his individuality.
While also wishing to have back
      my childish things.

MEN DON'T CRY

One day I fell, hurt myself, tears rolled uncontrollably; and my elders told me to shake it off. Be a man. They said be a man as if manhood is Instantaneous healing. It was as if Manhood erases pain from face and secures it in places only God knows. Does God even know?

                I'm trying.   Because
      Almost doesn't count,   *Real men* don't cry,
     No participation awards.   *Real men* just deal.
    Give 'til I'm breathless.   *Real men* supress how they feel.

Real men don't have depression.

                              Why do my feelings
                diminish because I'm breastless?

Real men's depression

                              Doesn't kill their sleep,
                                  Doesn't steal joy,
                          Doesn't murder innocence.

Real men don't have emotional issues
Real men don't have to heal.

                      It's their responsibility to be
                                     Good friend,
                                   Good brother,
                                     Good father,
                                        Good son.

                    Healing or not
         In a world all about Equal Rights,
          How I feel isn't equal, right?

Who says rape is only sexual? I ain't seen my innocence since adolescence. I learned then, the world's a judgemental place but speaking this is a woman's thing. *Real men* ain't 'sposed to worry, especially not about feelings 'til he realizes he has 'em.

Slim is the difference between boys and men, but big as existing is from living. Most never figure it out while living up to hyped stereotypes by a society that says displaying any form of humanity is a homosexual trait.

Tell them strength is recognition of imperfections and accepting them enough not to be crippled by them.

Sometimes I still feel pain in these scars.
Death been at my door so much he got a key.
He took loved ones
When I was waiting for him to come for me.
It would be easier that way.
'Til they say *Be a man.*

I'm black AND male, expected to be twice as strong. But how do I BE something I've been guessing at the whole damn time?

Tell me so I can stop crying.
Talk to me.

I don't want assumptions, no more old rhetoric of failed logic. Forget being nonchalant. It's done me no good. I've lived up to them the best I could. I still feel empty like Pinocchio but I'm too old to be a real boy. My ignorance is the only thing driving me 'til I find what I'm looking for.

If I'm ever supposed to know.

BIGGER THAN STANDARDS

I'm BIG.

You're probably thinking a guy my size is made just to eat. I hear it all the time. The sentiment is right, *kind of*. When it comes to enjoying life, I can't help but to salivate. I have *that* kind of appetite. One that finds joy in doing what works for me. Even if you think I ain't living right based on closed minded standards. Even if you think I should be happy with whatever I'm handed. What you may not know is:

I
- run like the wind blows.
- can look down and see all 10 toes
- don't have a big peen, I've got a great one.
- don't snore when I breathe
- got asthma but asthma don't got me.
- possess the swag of a man 100 pounds lighter.
- am my little one's superhero.
- am a fighter, not a biter.
- carry myself with dignity.
- sing rock and clap in unity.

And the only thing that moves me is my love, no lie. A love so large, this frame can barely contain. I've got so much of it that I can share it and still have surplus. Yes, sir plus!

So when you over critical, hypocritical, insecure, still trying to make good with genetics or whatever the fuck your parents chromosomes left you with people speak, know that you still can't buy, sell, nor trade the number of pounds you think are supposed to control my happiness to quench your misery.

I am much happier in this flawed chiseled sculpture. I count experiences, not my calories. I'm smiling while on the try it diet living gluttonous and free.

Well, because anything else would be small.

BEAR MY CROSS

God grant me serenity to accept the things I can't control and what I can, will be nothing less than my best.

I won't hide from secret counsels; I'm no secret. Give me strength to face Mufusa and Simba and walk out of the lion's den. I've been punching and kicking in the name of freedom aware that I'd be dumb if I want something free. But somebody upstairs already paid my fee.

I'm walking thru the valley of the shadow of death, but I ride or die with God: I'm never by myself. Even when I'm all alone, there's crazy calm in these psalms steady as the sword is in my palms.
>Protected while protective.
>I'll never take this armor off.

I'm prepared for the body blows and every tactic the enemy practices. In my defense, I give 'em my best shot: LeBron in Game 6.
>My table is set.
>On it?

Fried chicken, collard greens, sweet potatoes, hot water cornbread, macaroni, and cheese. Everything. So, bless this food which they are about to receive. I've been talked about, beat down, shot down, stabbed, and bent but not broken. Everything. I've been thru hell trying to get to heaven.

Knock me down but never will I epically fail. I got a best friend up there; He guards me well. The only way the west is won is if Thy will be done. Give me this day to soldier on. Though I don't move like I used to, I know the race isn't given to the swift nor the strong. I have learned to endure.

Not for the chapters I won't get to read, or the parables I'll never get to see, but for love. The kind of love that would star in the Book of Me when I'm not winning. When I'm valiantly sweating more than I've smiled, I will not fold. Never say die. That grave will be prepared for me one day, but not TODAY. I've got nations to change.

Placed on my brow is a fitted crown, pulled down, knowing that thru Christ, I can do ALL things. And that simple ornament sums all my scriptures to read one just thing:

King.

THE TRUTH ABOUT MY WORDS

*"Cause this life I live ain't for me, it's for you.
And God gave me grey clouds so your skies can be blue."*

A.B.Y.S.S Graham

I CAN'T

dear poetry,

its ME.
i feel like i owe you an apology.
sorry but

I CAN'T   be the poet everyone expects.
be the stereotypical, metaphysical, 3rd eye representation of a poet.
be the academic.
lie my way through.
be that which is not me.

i can only be the poet

I AM   the brutally honest, straight to the point, everyday struggle poet.

sorry but

NOBODY   can tell my story
can tell me how to tell my story
can relay the way i feel

i'm trying my damnedest to be **GOOD ENOUGH** not to be seen as just entertainment.
to be human.

i'm tired of feeling like
i'm a replay,
redundant,
salt on top of salty,
appalling.

      i just want to be beautiful to you.

dear poetry,

you are home.
i fail, and fail,
yet you still accept me.

the light's not always on but

THESE WORDS ARE candles, giving me hope
when i get lost in the shadows.
these words are band-aids,
helping me heal
when life is whipping my ass.

poetry,

thank you for being okay with me being me

THEN WHAT

Something that bothers me as a poet
Is the expectation to spit
Something black...

                                                                            Then what?

Do I become *more* black?
Like my reflection on rain drops
Hasn't made that evident?

Like I could possibly hide
This gorgeous hue of saddle brown
Anointed by God's grace and mercy.
My black is a reminder that
Even in pain,
                There's beauty.

I guess you wouldn't pay attention
'Cause I didn't say melanin
I hate the word melanin
Poets be talkin' slick
Sayin' seven letters like
It's a big word. Y'all weird.

Asians, Latinx,
Even those descendants from
The Caucuses got a bit.
It's just that we of African descent
Have so much of it,
Ours is called eumelanin.

But ain't that just like a nigga?
To wanna reduce something
so special to something simple.
I digress,
You want
                The "black thing".

Reciting a list
Of commonly known leaders
To seem knowledgeable.

Draped in ankhs
And Pan-African
For approval.

Poetically prostitute
As if my soul is
        Affordable.
As if ceiling is being
The next Martin, Malcolm,
        Rosa or Isabella.

Like the first me,
the first you
can't be better.
Like we ain't soldier in truth.
Afterall, greatness is measured
In tens. Tens. And tens.

We desecrate our dead
To win fucking
Poetry slams?

                                  AND THEN WHAT????

Did you at least send
Their mourning
Some of your winnings?

5 or 10 dollars
Entry fee not enough
For the price of their sacrifice?
You regurgitate
The details
However you choose.

It's necro-cannibalism
The way YouTube eats off
our loved ones for views.

                              Guess you want your portion too.

I will not. I rebel.
Stand strong. Empowered,
Clinched fist.

Make me the offer and I'll resist
The urge to be stereotypical.
Hypocritical.
I volunteer to assassinate agendas
Perpetuating propaganda
By associating press.

I can speak 'bout how it's
Going down in the hood but
Am I really doing my people good?
To bitch and whine
Over how a victim
               Died.

You can Google
Them yourself
And be more desensitized.
Not I.
But pull my black card and
This whole shit gets dark.

Rather than make you adore me
For the color of my skin,
I prefer to make you respect
How a barely high school graduate
Has become more impeccable
With the quality of his pen.

That's why I'm here.
It's the blackest thing
I know how to do.

NOVEMBER 18TH

Ethyl Jean Nelson passed peacefully in her sleep
November 18th, 2004.

She had a good day. She spent time with her daughter. She had her favorite dishes. Was granted all her wishes. And I had to hear about it. Because I had slept that day away after an argument.

When she passed.
They gave me 3 days for bereavement. I took off more and celebrated Thanksgiving the next week. And that's supposed to be enough time to get over it. I tried liquor, weed, sex. Things to take my mind off what I was dealing with...

So why so many years later am I still fucked up about it?

I can hardly give Total Praise with a straight face. I prefer to work Thanksgiving Day rather than to fix a plate and not see my grandmother's face. A glass of her favorite eggnog can't replace the pain. I gave my daughter her name to give her a connection with her.

My grandmother didn't get to see herself become a great grandmother to 2 of the most beautiful little girls I'll ever know. I get so sick analyzing that day. I ask myself why I couldn't have given her orchids? Or maybe, long stem roses? Why didn't I go say I'm sorry? I meant what I said because I love hard, I just wanted things to be okay. Why did I have to be so foolish and stupid speaking in ways unbecoming of the boy she helped raise?

Give or take it's been:
14 years.
5110 days.
122,640 hours.
7,358,400 minutes.
441,504,000...1, 2, 3 seconds and counting...

But still not enough time for the hole in my heart to vanish. Telling me it'll be ok, to me, is a foreign form, Spanish. I lack patience to translate. Some days, when life is really hard, I go to your room, wait on your bed for you to come in. I am waiting for you to provide a hug that exorcises my nightmares. But you still haven't come.

I guess you're gone even in my dreams.

Your eldest grandkid has done a lot and seen more. I've made history and still haven't conquered this demon that's been giving me hell since you left. I'd give everything back just for one more hug, one more kiss, one more chance to say I'm sorry. You should have been given all your flowers while you were still here.

All I have now is time.
And more time is not the answer to my problem.

BIO

Brandon "Amayzn" Nelson is a decorated spoken word artist known for his impactful, down to earth, high-energy delivery. Born and raised Kansas City, Missouri, he has dedicated his talents to reaching those often looked over by academic speakers. From his point of view the connection to people is more important than being technically correct or talking over their heads.

Amayzn is also a vocalist, radio personality, mentor, and host. He has shared the stage with many greats, having his work recorded and distributed to the masses. He is also a competitive poet having had the opportunity to represent Kansas City nationally and winning many competitions locally.

- amayzn816
- amayznkc
- amayzn

www.ingramcontent.com/pod-product-compliance
Lightning Source LLC
Chambersburg PA
CBHW050336120526
44592CB00014B/2211